D0090310

A Little Book of

IRISH SUPERSTITIONS

Kim Lenaghan
Illustrated by David McAllister

Appletree Press

First published in 1995 by
Appletree Press Ltd
The Old Potato Station
14 Howard Street South
Belfast BT7 1AP
Tel: +44 (0) 28 90 243074
Fax: +44 (0) 28 90 246756
Web site: www.appletree.ie
Email: reception@appletree.ie

A Little Book of Irish Superstitions

A catalogue record for this book
is available from the British Library.

ISBN 0 86281-545-2

9 8 7 6 5 4 3 2

CONTENTS

INTRODUCTION

No doubt about it, the Irish have always been very superstitious. Of course, every country has its folk customs and superstitions, but Ireland does seem to have more than most. Even a brief look back in history, particularly in rural areas, will reveal a pattern for daily living that was hugely influenced by the superstitious beliefs of the community.

These superstitions took many forms: spells, potions, incantations, cures, charms, omens and rituals. They were said to have the power to heal the sick, help the lovelorn, predict good and bad luck, ward off evil, and much more. No-one really knows where they came from or how they came about, but they appear to contain a mix of Christianity, naturalism, folklore and social history in liberal measures.

The obvious fact of coincidence doesn't seem to figure at all. Human nature being what it is, people looked for a cause for things they couldn't understand or explain and leapt to some conclusion, generally the wrong one.

Take fishermen and sailors who were, and still are, particularly superstitious. They were battling against natural elements beyond man's control, yet some human explanation for accidents and events at sea still had to be sought as a justification. If a fisherman was drowned it couldn't possibly be the result of a storm, or lack of care. No, it would be more likely that someone on board was whistling, an act considered the most ill of omens. We can only assume that superstitions like this grew up because once or twice, at some point in history, a whistling seaman coincided with a drowning. So an unhappy coincidence becomes a superstition enshrined in the general belief system of a community.

Ultimately, the one thing all superstitions had in common was that they were concerned chiefly with the helplessness of the human condition. In times of trouble, crisis or illness people would turn to these old superstitions and remedies which might not have cured or helped them but faith in their ability to work brought comfort, whether real or imagined. There was the idea, too, of tradition and the familiarity of continuing the old ways.

Many of these superstitions have died out in the face of modern living and it is hard to tell how widely practised any of them might be today. As to whether or not they might still work, I'll leave it to you to decide.

GOOD OMENS

What was considered a good omen and why? Again, it seems that there is no explanation other than that of coincidence.

Sometimes the same things could actually represent both good and bad omens, depending on how the signs were read. For example, black cats who crossed your path were a lucky sign, but the first person seen by a cat that wiped its face with its paws would be the first in the household to die.

It was considered very lucky for a hen and her chicks to stray into your house, or to meet a white lamb in the early morning with the sunlight on its face. This, however, would not have been an omen familiar to the average city dweller.

Better still if you found the back tooth of a horse and carried it with you every day of your life; you would never want for money. A note of caution though, as this only worked if you happened upon the tooth by accident. A foolish – or some might say brave – man who deliberately extracted a tooth from a horse's mouth for luck would gain nothing.

A purse made from the skin of a weasel would never be empty of money. But the purse must be found, not made or given. I have looked at some length for a weasel skin wallet in the hopes of proving this theory but as yet have had little success.

If you heard a cuckoo on your right side you would have luck all the year after, and the shoe of a horse or donkey nailed to the door-post would bring continuing good fortune to a house. This was thought to be because these animals were in the stall when Christ was born and so were blessed for evermore. But, as always, the shoe must be found, not given; it seems that the Irish had little belief in making your own luck.

Any dream involving horses was thought to be very lucky and even to dream of a hearse being drawn by plumed horses was a good omen foretelling a wedding. Strangely enough, to actually dream of a wedding had quite the opposite effect and was considered very bad news indeed. Whatever their content, dreams were never revealed before the dreamer's fast was broken and, if possible, first told to a girl called Mary.

Walking around a card table could change a player's luck if the walking was conducted in a sunwise direction and provided the sun was shining on the opponent's hand. Naturally, this applied only to card games played in daylight hours, a most disreputable practice.

When a servant girl left her place of employ, if her mistress gave her a piece of bread and she put some of it carefully away, as long as she kept it good luck would follow her.

The wearing of a crooked pin in the lapel was thought likely to bring about good fortune. A four-leaf clover ensured luck in gambling and racing, but must always be carried and never shown.

Even today, it is still considered very lucky for a bride to see a chimney sweep on the way to her wedding. Perhaps the lack of chimney sweeps in the late twentieth century goes some way to explaining the rise in marital break-ups.

ILL OMENS

Many omens were prophecies of bad luck or ill fortune, and for obvious reasons there were many more of these than good omens. Some were natural phenomena and indicators of ill fate which could not be altered, others gave a warning of danger or mishap which should be heeded.

It was dicing with death to cross in the path of a plough and horses, and perhaps the modern equivalent would be to run in the path of a large tractor ploughing a field. It was also considered tempting fate to steal a plough or take anything by stealth from a smith's forge.

If a chair fell before you rose from it, that indicated some sort of misfortune to follow, and if for no apparent reason a picture fell off the wall it foretold a death in the family within the year.

Three candles should never be lit at once and left in a room, and it was even more unlucky to put out a candle or lamp while people were at supper for surely there would be one less sitting at the table by that time the following year.

On the way to or from a funeral you would never buy or sell an animal as this was considered not just the height of bad manners but an open invitation to bad luck. The same ill fortune would follow if you met with a funeral on the road and did not walk back three steps with it.

No self-respecting Irish man or woman would ever have cut their toenails on a Sunday. This was because evil witches lurking nearby could use these clippings to cast wicked spells on them.

You would never even think of mending a tear in a dress while wearing it, or evil and malicious reports would be spread about you.

You were in for a really rough time if you happened to pass under a rope made of hemp. Any person unfortunate enough to do so would die a violent death, or be fated to commit some act of unspeakable evil in later life.

If one magpie came chattering to your door and looked at you, it was another sure death-sign and nothing could avert the doom. But among fatal signs the most fatal was to break a looking-glass, for as well as the usual seven years bad luck, it was thought certain that someone in the house would die before the year was out and again there was no way to avoid this dread fate.

It was unlucky to accept a lock of hair or a four-footed beast from a lover, and you would never offer your left hand in greeting to a friend because of the old saying: "A curse with the left hand to those we hate, but the right hand to those we honour."

When moving house it was inadvisable to bring a cat with you, especially across a stream, and a red and white cat was particularly ominous. If a black cat came of its own accord to your new house you should keep it for it was certain to be a good spirit.

The new moon was treated with much suspicion and if it was

first seen through glass, it would be most unlucky. To prevent the loss of luck you would turn over the change in your pocket and bow to the moon seven times.

Whoever killed a robin redbreast would never have good luck were they to live for a thousand years. The likely reason for this was thought to be that the robin was God's own bird for it plucked out the sharpest thorn piercing Christ's brow. In doing so, the breast of the bird was dyed red with the Saviour's blood and it has remained so ever since as a blessed sign to preserve the robin from harm and make it beloved of all men.

Consider, too, the fate that would befall you if you happened upon a red-haired woman on your way to work. Surprisingly, in a Celtic country that boasts many such women, this was thought to be very unlucky indeed. The only way to avoid your ill fate

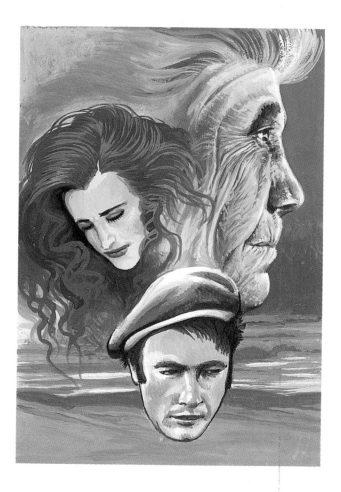

was to return home for the day. Similarly, if a man on his way to work was asked where he was going, he would again be inclined to go back home to avoid some catastrophe. Evidence as to whether or not this was merely a convenient excuse for many a work-shy Irishman is inconclusive.

A tale from Rostrevor in County Down, Northern Ireland, tells of a farm in the area that was thought to be very unlucky. No matter what was done, crops never prospered, and the livestock sickened and died. One day, while the farmer was working in the fields, an old woman came to him claiming she could rid him of his bad luck if he did exactly what she said. She went with him to the house where he was instructed to get a pot of nails, fill it with water and put it on the fire. Next he had to bar the door so no-one could enter and churn butter while the nails boiled in their pot. When they were bubbling and spitting on the fire a thunderous knocking was heard at the door and the old woman told the farmer to open it. There on the threshold was a red-haired women wailing in pain "For pity's sake take the nails off the fire for I can stand it no longer." He lifted off the pot, the two women disappeared, and from that day onward the farm prospered.

But it wasn't just red-haired women who were bad omens, men with red hair were also treated with great suspicion, and it is thought that this mistrust stemmed from the widely held belief that Judas Iscariot, who betrayed Jesus after the Last Supper, was a red-head.

Another old superstition thought to have biblical roots, was that a boy's hair should never be cut by a woman. It seems probable

that this was linked to the Old Testament story of Samson and Delilah.

You always had to leave a house by the same door you entered it or you would take the good luck from there with you. For the same reason you would never brush crumbs from the kitchen floor to the outside.

It was considered very unlucky to meet a barefooted man or whistling woman, or for two people to wash their hands in a basin at the same time. Opening an umbrella indoors and placing new shoes, a cap or a hat on the table would be courting disaster.

Eggshells would never be burned on the fire as this was thought to draw sickness to the house, and under no circumstances should you ever return borrowed salt.

A crowing hen was very unlucky and would be killed, most

often stoned to death, for it was believed that the hen was bewitched by the fairies. You would bring some terrible punishment on yourself, though, if you killed an old heron or a swan for these were thought to be the spirits of old people, bewitched by supernatural forces.

One omen for the gardeners is that extreme bad luck was certain to follow if you transplanted parsley from your vegetable patch unless it was to give to someone else. If you gave it away then any misfortune would be avoided.

Whilst a weasel wallet would never be empty, it was thought extreme bad luck to meet with a live weasel, and worse still if you actually killed the creature, for the whole family of the murdered weasel would take vengeance on you before the year was out. The only way to avoid your ill fate would be to kill one of your hens, pray over it and leave it hanging on a post.

LOVE AND MARRIAGE

This provided limitless scope for spells, potions and superstitions, with desperate young maidens going to extreme lengths to catch eligible bachelors or to identify the man they would marry.

Ways to predict Mr. Right ranged from eating an apple while looking in a mirror on Halloween Night to see his shadowy reflection in the glass, to gathering snails at dawn on May Day and placing them on a dish of flour to watch them make a trail that would spell the name of the husband to be.

Not all the ways to foretell love were quite as easy as this, and girls often had to go to some elaborate lengths to reveal the identity of their future partner. The following rhyme would be recited by a maiden as she gathered herbs by the light of the first full moon of the New Year:

> "Moon, Moon tell unto me
> When my true love I will see.
> What fine clothes am I to wear?
> How many children will I bear?
> For if my love comes not to me,
> Dark and dismal my life will be."

Then, with a black-handled knife, she would cut three pieces of earth, bring them home, tie them in her left stocking with her right garter and sleep with the bundle under her pillow.

Kale, a kind of cabbage, seems to have been accepted as a good predictor of a girl's chances in the marriage stakes. If she went out to the cabbage patch and pulled out a runt of kale and it had plenty of soil on it then her future husband would have a good farm of land. But this prediction would only come true if she then threw the runt over the roof.

Another spell involved stealing a kale stock from someone else's garden at midnight on the eve of Halloween. The girl would fasten this stock over the door to her home and the first man to enter in the morning would have the same first name as her future husband. In small rural communities where particular names like Michael and John were commonly used it is easy to see how this practice was believed.

If a girl wanted to dream of her future lover she could steal a salt herring and eat it without taking a drink before going to bed. On the night before May Day twelve stalks of yarrow placed under the pillow would have the same effect and be a lot less thirsty work.

In the Kilkeel area of County Down, Northern Ireland, it was considered a powerful spell if before going to bed for the night a girl sprinkled the four corners of her mattress with salt, saying as she did:

"Salt, salt I salt thee
In the name of God in unity.
If I'm for a man
Or a man for me
In my first sleep
May I him see.
The colour of his hair
The clothes he'll wear
The day he'll wed with me."

Once he was identified, apparently one of the best ways to catch an eligible young man was to use a potion concocted from the ground liver of a black cat. When infused this was such a powerful aphrodisiac that a man under its spell would be so carried away with desire that they would promise the girl anything, including a binding proposal of marriage.

Another method of entrapment, again not for animal lovers, used the bones of a frog that had been buried alive in a box in a ditch. When the frog had died and the flesh withered, the maiden would select a bone, secrete it about the person of the object of her desire and he would then be completely captivated.

It sounds radical and, certainly, you would want to have the dosage right, but ground hemlock added to food or drink was believed to make a man return unrequited love. If a young woman was in doubt as to whom exactly the hemlock should be administered, she had only to throw a ball of wool into the lime kiln and wind it up until an invisible hand held it tight. If she then asked who held the wool a voice would tell her the name of her future husband.

A rather gruesome, but thought to be most effective love charm was for a young girl to take a piece of skin from the arm of a corpse, place it under her pillow and her future husband would appear in her dreams. If she was to tie it on the man whose love she sought while he lay sleeping, and remove it before he awoke, then as long as the girl kept the skin she would retain his love, no matter what. But the use of this spell was not without its risks.

Legend has it that a young girl who was a servant to a rich family tried this charm thinking she might dream of one of the other staff or a boy from the village. The next morning the lady of the house asked her what she had dreamed of, and the girl replied anxiously that she had dreamt of her master.

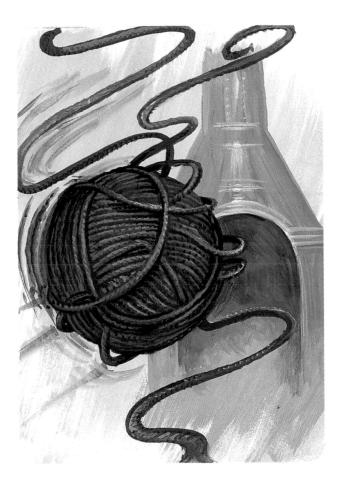

No more was thought of it until a few months later when the lady died suddenly. The servant girl, remembering her dream, waited for an opportunity to remove some skin from a recent corpse and tied it around her master as he slept. After he woke he became entirely infatuated with the girl and married her although she was low-born and rather plain.

He adored his new wife for a year and a day until there was a fire in the house, and the strip of skin the girl had kept carefully hidden in her room was burnt. Immediately the magic charm was broken and her husband saw all her faults and the unsuitability of their marriage. To his horror she confessed what she had done, and so greatly was she shunned and despised for her evil spell that she died half mad within the year.

Fortunately, the young men being hunted for husbands were

not entirely defenceless. They could ward off unwanted attentions by acquiring a lock of hair from the infatuated female in question, burning it, and eating the ashes scattered on their food.

If, however, a young man wished to bind a woman to him, he would keep a sprig of mint in his hand until it was moist, then take hold of her hand and both must stay silent for ten minutes. She would then follow him anywhere as long as their hands were joined, and presumably she would be so enamoured of him by the time they had to separate that she would then stay of her own accord.

If a man wanted to dream of his future wife, as so many young girls wished to dream of a husband, there was only one month in the year when he got the chance. In November he would take a distaff – the cleft stick used to hold wool or flax wound for spinning – place it under his head at night and he would dream of the girl he was destined to marry.

All these spells were important because spinsters and confirmed bachelors of the parish received rather a hard time.

Traditionally no marriages could take place in the period over Lent, so if you hadn't got yourself a wife or a husband by Shrove Tuesday you'd missed your chance until after Easter. People in the country loved nothing better than a good wedding and if you cheated them out of it they could get quite disgruntled. This ire was particularly directed at those men and women of marriageable age who remained stubbornly unwed year after year offering no prospect of a good wedding feast. So on Shrove Tuesday night, when the marriage season was over for a while, these poor spinsters and bachelors were singled out for attention. Pranks played on them included everything from the blocking up of their chimneys to having the hinges taken off their gates and the wheels removed from their carts.

Worst treatment of all came in County Waterford, where on Ash Wednesday the unfortunate unmarrieds of the town were tied to a large log and dragged along the quayside whilst offensive graffiti was scrawled on the doors of their houses. Fortunately, this practice has long since died out.

If someone pipped you to the post and got the partner you wanted you could cause hatred between the lovers by taking a handful of clay from a new-made grave and shaking it between them saying: "Hate ye one another! May ye be as hateful to each other as sin to Christ, as bread eaten without blessing is to God."

If you wanted to ensure a long and happy union, however, you would offer your betrothed a drink over which the following incantation was said: "You for me and I for thee and no-one else, your face to mine and your head turned away from all others."

If the happy couple ever actually made it to the altar there were a number of important superstitions and traditions to be borne in mind.

Those who married in autumn would die in spring, and a girl should never get married during the harvest or she would have no rest from worries and troubles, and would always be overworked and laden with cares and anxieties throughout her life. It seems somewhat unlikely, however, that this care-ridden life would have been reserved only for harvest brides.

On their wedding day a new-married couple should always retire to rest at the same time, for if the bride were left alone the fairies would come and steal her away for the sake of her fine clothes. But a new bride was thought to have powers over the fairies unless she happened to take both feet off the floor in a dance, and then she would lose that power.

The bride's home would never be re-entered by her or her new husband until a month had passed.

One very romantic rural custom had the groom presenting his new bride with some golden butter on a newly made dish, beside a mill, a tree or a stream and saying: "Oh woman, loved by me, mayest thou give me thy heart, thy soul and thy body."

BIRTH AND DEATH

Many omens, prophecies and superstitions surround the coming into and leaving of life, the biggest events in the human calendar.

A particularly vindictive enemy could prevent a couple conceiving a child by tying a knot in a handkerchief at the time of their marriage. No child would be born to that couple until this knot was loosed.

Perhaps this childless pair might have taken heed of some of the following handy hints. A woman would almost certainly become pregnant if a child looked at her from between its legs. If she sat on a seat just vacated by a pregnant woman or tried on her coat then the pregnancy would be "catching".

In County Tyrone there was a tradition that said if a woman of child-bearing age was in the company of two pregnant women she too would become pregnant unless she prevented it by quickly slapping her backside three times.

If a pregnant woman accidentally met with a hare her child might be born with a harelip. If she did encounter such a creature she would tear the hem of her dress thereby transferring the blemish to it. Even a hare already killed by a hunter could cause this condition in a baby if the hare's tail had not been removed before being brought into the presence of an expectant mother.

For a similar reason, a pregnant woman would never enter a graveyard lest she turn her ankle and cause her child to be born with a clubfoot. This could, however, be counteracted by throwing a handful of graveyard clay at the woman in question. Another superstition suggested that if she attended a funeral, or even met with one by chance, she would have a miscarriage or her baby would be still-born.

When the time for the actual birth arrived difficult confinements often called for the presence of a seventh son who would shake the patient roughly three times. If a seventh son wasn't available then any man not married to a red-haired woman would do. It must have been the last thing the poor woman needed, to be shaken to bits by any passing farmer.

The custom of *couvade* was practised widely in Ireland, whereby it was hoped to lessen the worst pains of childbirth for the mother by transferring some of them to the father. It was usual for a woman about to give birth to wear a waistcoat or some other item of clothing belonging to her husband. An alternative form of the practice was for the father to do some special type of work until the baby was born. In County Longford he often had the duty of carrying a heavy flagstone around the house during the labour.

There are all sorts of stories about the luck of a child born with a caul. This is a membrane which on rare occasions is found around the child when it is delivered. In such a case, the caul was preserved by the mother and as long as she kept it the child would never drown.

A first-born child would never be rocked in a new cradle and, if an infant died at birth, it was thought that the mother would never have another child if the lid was nailed on the coffin. Babies who died unbaptised were not buried in consecrated ground but laid to rest at the boundaries of graveyards.

The most inauspicious time for any birth was Whitsuntide. A rather gruesome fate was in store for any children born then for it was believed that they would grow up either to become killers or themselves be killed. This disastrous prophecy would be unfulfilled if a live worm was put into the infant's hand and crushed until dead. For the same reason, it was also a common practice for these babies to be briefly laid in a specially dug grave.

If Whitsun was an unlucky time to be born then May Day was the complete opposite and humans or even animals born on that day were said to be assured of good luck. At no time, though, was it considered a lucky omen to have three people born in any house in the same month.

Whatever time of year the moment of birth took place it had to be when all the cupboards in the house were open. These were immediately locked as soon as the child was born lest the fairies would get in and hide, awaiting their chance to steal the infant.

It was firmly believed, despite the most vigilant care, that the fairies were always trying to take away a newly-born baby, or woman in child-birth who would nurse the infants in fairyland. It was thought that those who sickened or wasted away had actually been taken by the fairies who left sickly changelings behind in their place. Elaborate precautions were taken to protect both mothers and babies from this abduction. These included oatmeal being given to the mother as soon as the baby was born: a piece of iron or a cinder concealed in the baby's dress; the fire tongs placed across the cradle; unsalted butter in the baby's mouth; a red ribbon tied across the cradle and many other similar talismans.

A childless woman who stared at another's child too intently was to be treated with great caution. The "evil-eye" could spirit away an infant.

There is a story of a woman in County Galway who had a child so beautiful that everyone who saw him would say "God bless it" for they knew the fairies would want to steal him away. But one day an old woman called by the house and asked if she could come in and rest. She stared fixedly at the child in strange silence but never blessed him and after a few minutes she went on her way.

All that night and the next the child cried, moaning with pain, and would not sleep. When his mother was in complete despair over what to do she saw a wise-looking old lady going by the door and decided to ask for her help. She asked her to come in and rest, and the old lady looked at the child saying "God bless it" and spat three times, and the mother knew then she was right and good. The old woman explained that the fairies had taken the child and left a changeling in its place, but so many blessings had been said on the child that no real harm could come to him. Only one blessing had been denied and that was from the woman who had fixed him with the "evil-eye". The only remedy was to watch for the woman, bring her into the house, secretly cut off a piece of her cloak and burn it beside the child until the smoke made him sneeze; then the spell would be broken and her child returned.

The next day the evil woman appeared once again and, as instructed, the mother brought her into the house for supper and while she was eating cut a piece from her cloak. When the woman had gone, the mother burned the cloth beside the infant until he sneezed and then placed him in bed where he finally slept. When he awoke smiling and laughing the other knew she had her own child back safe and sound, despite the "evil-eye".

There are still many customs and practices surrounding death and burial in Ireland. Many omens are to foretell impending death, though in reality this was more likely to be determined by the rapidly declining health of the patient.

Nine magpies seen together meant a death in the townland and four together meant a death in the house nearest to them. To dream of the loss of an eye tooth was a sure sign of death, as was dreaming of a cabbage.

Birds perched on the window-sill of the sick room or a raven seen flying over the house were sure signs of death and, if a dog howled at night or a cock was heard to crow after dusk, then you could expect a corpse by morning. However, the most eerie warning of all was the strange, unnatural wailing of that legendary Irish prophetess of doom, the *bean si* (Banshee), of whom more later.

The clocks were always stopped at the moment of death, a custom still practised in some rural areas, and the mirrors in the house veiled. There was a tradition, too, that if bees were kept they had to be told the sad news and the hive draped in black.

It was thought lucky to die at Christmas or, rather, if you had to die at all Christmas was the best time for it. It was said that during the twelve days of Christmas the gates of heaven were open for all to enter. It was also a popular belief that men met death quietly while women resisted it.

When the body in its coffin was removed from the house where it had been laid out, it was placed for a few moments on chairs. These were immediately knocked down when the coffin was lifted onto the shoulders of the bearers, who should be four men of the same surname as the deceased.

A funeral was a time to get dressed up in your best clothes, but it was considered not just disrespectful but highly unlucky to wear anything new to a funeral.

The connection between death and water was a strong one and water was thought to keep any restless spirit from returning to haunt the living. For this reason, many Irish funerals took a route to the graveyard that passed over a river or stream. Customarily, the funeral cortège stopped at any crossroads for prayers or if it passed by the house of the deceased. If by chance the funeral procession met a man riding a grey horse there would be another death in the same family in the near future.

Grave-diggers left their spades and shovels crossed above an open grave or four twigs would be crossed at either end of its base. When the coffin arrived, it was carried around this cross three times before being lowered. If a clumsy pallbearer accidentally dropped the corpse, dire consequences would follow and, if one of the mourners stumbled by the graveside, it was considered very unlucky, though not as unlucky as if they actually fell and touched the clay from the grave.

An old custom in Longford was never to wipe your boots in a graveyard, while in Galway it was said that if you lost something in a graveyard you should never look for it.

In many places it was normal for a young married woman who died to be buried with her own people and not in the grave of her husband's family. The belief was that if the husband married again it would make for a very unquiet grave if he had two wives in it.

But of all the superstitions that surrounded death the most macabre custom was "the touch of the dead". The woman of the house where a death had occurred would stir milk with the hand of the corpse, and this was believed to increase the butter yield. One legend tells how a woman who cut off the hand of a dead body to use at churning time was later visited from beyond the grave by the corpse in question and forced to take the hand with her to the graveyard every night for a month to beg for forgiveness.

Fairies, Spirits and Banshees

airies and spirits who roam the countryside figure very largely in Irish superstition. While there has always been some scepticism among Irish country people about the existence of fairies and the like, there has nonetheless been a healthy respect shown to the possibility. This stems from the need to give some explanation, however unlikely, to the otherwise inexplicable.

The fairies had many names in Irish meaning "The Good People", "The Noble People", "The People Outside Us" and, best known of all, "The Little People". It was widely believed that these fairies were in fact fallen angels, or spirits in limbo, not evil enough to be sent to hell or good enough for heaven.

Generally these fairies were of human appearance, except of course for the fabled Irish leprechaun. They lived in forts and farmed and kept cattle like their human counterparts. They were famous for their revelries and enjoyed nothing better than to feast, dance and make music which was said to have an enchanting effect on mortals. They were thought to be at the height of their powers in November and a red-haired man, always an object of earthly mistrust, could assist a mortal in the fairyworld.

They also loved horseracing and were said to have an eye for a beautiful woman. If a fairy male actually took a mortal bride and their children didn't come up to his exacting standards they would be summarily returned to live among the humans and a suitable replacement stolen on the journey back to the fairy kingdom. But most children from the union between fairies and mortals were not only beautiful but very musical, and with a wild and reckless temperament.

If you suspected that you saw one of these fairies up to some devilment, then a hat, a wedding dress or a left shoe should be thrown in their direction. But, of course, you could only see a fairy if you had been born in the evening; a person born in the morning would never see one.

It was on Fridays that the fairies were thought to have the most influence over human fate and so for that reason Friday was a bad day to begin work, go on a journey, or have a wedding. On that day the fairies could see and hear everything that was going on and attempt to spoil it out of spite and jealousy for the mortal race. It was then they were most likely to strike down cattle with their elfin arrows, steal the milk and carry off handsome children. For obvious reasons great care was taken to keep on the "right side" of fairy neighbours.

Crumbs that dropped from the table were often left for "them", and it was generally thought that fairies were good to mortals who observed the superstitions of leaving them food and pails of water to bathe with. In return for such kindness the fairies might reward these humans with some of their golden apples, words of wisdom, swords of knowledge or bottles of wine that could never be emptied.

Finvarra, king of the fairies of the west, was on good terms with most of the best families in Galway, and especially with the Kirwans of Castle Hacket. In thanks for the family leaving out kegs of fine Spanish wine for him at night, he was said to return the compliment be ensuring the wine cellars of the castle were never empty, though wine and hospitality flowed freely for all.

It was a foolish man who would knowingly build on the site of a "fairy fort", or on one of the "passes" that led from one fort to another. This was one of the chief ways to cause the fairies offence and the consequences could be dire. Mortals seldom knew the whereabouts of fairy land but they would know soon enough if they started to build on it. If there was any doubt, the foundations for a house would be dug and left overnight to see if they were filled in, or a fairy emissary might be sent to offer some gift, like lifelong prosperity, if the building was erected elsewhere.

The fairies were blamed for all sorts of inexplicable illnesses, and when a human died suddenly and without warning it was often ascribed to a "fairy blast" or said to be a "fairy stroke".

There were many other spirits, generally evil, who were thought to inhabit the earth after death as punishment for some awful crime committed during their human life. This sentence was eternal and it was believed that this was what prompted their resentment toward the mortals they met late at night.

Spirits could be both male and female, but females were considered the more formidable. These spirits could be conquered or banished by employing such devices as holy water, a black-handled knife, an iron chain or a hazel stick. Priests were particularly successful in getting rid of spirits by banishing them to some narrow place such as between the bark and the wood of a tree. If pursued at night by an evil spirit or a ghost of the dead the best way to escape their evil clutches was to try and reach a stream of running water and cross it, for they would be quite unable to follow.

Of all Irish spirits the most widely known is the *bean si*

(Banshee), an omen and prophecy of death from which there was no escape. Seldom seen but always heard, she was said to cry forth a bloodcurdling, supernatural wail near the home of one who was about to die. When the family heard the sound they knew with certainty that one of them was soon to be deceased.

The Banshee did not cry to every household and it was believed she appeared most to old, aristocratic families. She was also thought to be particularly fond of families with musical talents and if she attached herself to a particular family she would follow them to the ends of the earth.

This certainly appeared to be the case with some members of the O'Grady clan. One branch had settled in Canada, far away from all the superstitious beliefs and influences of their homeland. Yet one night a bitter, unearthly cry full of the deepest agony and sorrow was heard outside their house, though no-one was seen. The next day the master and his eldest son went out boating and by dinner time had still not returned. Then, at precisely the same hour that the cry had been heard the previous evening, the bodies of the father and son, who had been drowned in an accident, were carried up the driveway to the house. The prophecy of the Banshee had been fulfilled and she was heard no more.

The Banshee would appear as a beautiful young girl with long red-gold hair or at other times shrouded and muffled in a cloak. There was no harm or fear of evil in her mere presence, the problem was only if she started to cry. She was reputed to spend her spare time, in between wails, attending to her coiffure.

HIGH DAYS AND HOLIDAYS

Much superstition and custom was attached to special days in the year. These centred around the rites and beliefs of both the old pagan feasts and the newer Christian holidays.

For obvious reasons some of the best examples were associated with Halloween, when the dead came back to haunt the living and the fairies were abroad. As has already been described, this was a key occasion in the year for identifying potential husbands, and yet another custom for predicting the outcome of love on Halloween night came from the placing of pairs of chestnuts by the open fire to represent an engaged couple. These would be seriously scrutinised and, if they stayed together on being heated, the couple would live together in harmony, but if they scattered there would be much strife.

It was also thought that if you washed some item of your clothing in a running brook on Halloween, hung it on a thorn bush and then waited, you would see a vision of your future lover come to turn the washing on the bush.

All spells carried out on that night were thought to be in the name of the devil and so carried a certain risk. One story has it that on Halloween a young servant girl was trying out a spell in front of the mirror to find a lover, but it went wrong and she saw something too horrible to reveal to anyone, and the girl was certain she would die. The other staff in the house tried to calm her fears by laughing it off, but sure enough, the next night she was found lying dead on the floor in front of the mirror with her face horribly contorted and the glass shattered in pieces around her.

Naturally at this time there were many supposed predictors of death, including knocking over a candle on Halloween which was considered a very ill omen. Small piles of salt were often placed on a plate, one to represent each member of the family. A pile that caved in signified death within the year for that person.

At Halloween people avoided taking shortcuts across beaches, fields or cliffs for fear the fairies would lead them astray. Worse still would happen if you were out walking on the last night of November, the official closing of the fairy season of merriment. This was the night for the dead to have their fling; dancing with the fairies on the hillsides and drinking their potent wine. After that they would return to rest in their coffins until the following November.

As well as the traditional celebrations with the yule log, holly and candles, the season of Christmas was seen as another festival for honouring the dead and predicting the future. In parts of County Donegal on the twelfth night after Christmas, a round cake was placed on the kitchen table and candles, one to represent each member of the family, pushed into it and lit. The candles were said to go out in order of the deaths of the family members.

It was believed too that on Christmas morning the donkey would kneel down in adoration of Christ and in remembrance of His birth in the stable. If you could touch the cross on the back of the animal at that particular moment the wish of your heart would be granted, whatever it was.

On Christmas morning it was also thought very lucky to breakfast by candlelight, and on Stephen's Day, the day after Christmas, it was believed that if you fasted and no flesh was eaten that it would leave the entire family immune to all infectious diseases in the coming year.

On New Year's Day you would never give away money or milk for fear of losing good fortune for the year. For the same reason no ashes or even crumbs from the floor would be swept from the house lest the luck go with them.

In a Christian country like Ireland it was considered very unlucky to use a hammer and nails on Good Friday, the day of Christ's crucifixion. No meat should be hung on a nail that day, no blood shed and no milk drunk. All cakes baked had the sign of the cross put upon them, and in Ireland today there is still a

widespread tradition of baking and eating "hot cross buns", a spicy currant bread, in the period around Easter.

Not only was Whitsuntide, the fiftieth day after Easter (Pentecost in the church calendar) a most unlucky time to be born. It was also a day associated with drowning and many sailors would only set sail that day if their vessel was being steered by the steady hand of a new bride who was thought to have special powers over the sea and could not be harmed by it. It was also ill advised to go on a journey where a stream or river had to be crossed, or even to bathe on that day.

A candle should never be lit without making the sign of the cross over the flame to ward off evil, and if anyone took ill at Whitsuntide there was great danger of death as evil spirits were out on watch to carry off victims. Therefore no sick person would be left alone or in the dark at that time.

May Day was one of the most important annual festivals in Ireland and marked the beginning of the summer when prosperity for the year ahead would be determined by healthy livestock and good produce.

The first three days of May were very dangerous to cattle for it was believed the fairies had a power over them so they were well guarded by lighted fires and branches of the rowan, and the milkmaid made the sign of the cross after milking with the froth of the milk. On the eve of May Day cattle were driven into Cooey Bay off Devenish Island to prevent their developing the cattle disease "murrain". The fairies could also have a very detrimental effect on butter and cream.

At any time of year the giving away of milk was ill advised, but this was particularly the case on May Day. Tradition had it that whoever first got the milk of a certain cow that day received the profit from the cow for the rest of the year. This custom was so well established that one court of law even acquitted a farmer who on May Day assaulted an intruder in his barn believing him to be after the milk.

Another popular tradition on May Day was to decorate around the cottage doors and windows with primroses and whins to keep away the fairies. But it was considered highly unlucky to bring hawthorn into the house as this was believed to form the crown of thorns which Christ wore on his crucifixion.

Pipes were never lit from the glowing embers of a fire nor were these embers ever carried outside on May Day lest the luck go with them. If the fire went out on May Day morning it was considered very unlucky and it could not be re-kindled except by using a lighted sod brought from the priest's house.

Before sunrise, country people would cut hazel rods from which they carved small figures to ward off evil, and ashes were often scattered on the threshold. If a footprint was found in these ashes in the morning, and it turned inwards, it predicted a marriage; if, however, it turned outwards it foretold a death. A red-headed woman, never exactly popular at other times of the year, would not be let over the threshold on May Day lest she bring a curse on the house.

The fairies also had a habit on May Eve of stealing children or young men and women to be fairy husbands and brides. Therefore, no door was left open after sunset and no-one would sleep outside.

There is a story of one young man who died suddenly on May Eve while asleep under a haystack. Everyone immediately guessed that he must have been carried off by the fairies, so a man renowned for dealing with these spirits was sent for. He promised to have the young man back within nine days if each night food and drink was left for him by his family. This was done and the food always disappeared so it was believed he was still alive. On the ninth night a great crowd assembled to see him brought back from Fairyland, and in the middle of the gathering was the man performing his incantations and throwing powder on a fire. Then taking off his hat and holding a key in his hand he called out three times "Come forth, come forth, come forth!" With that a shrouded figure appeared and the voice of the young man was heard to say "Leave me in peace; I am happy with my fairy bride, and my family need not weep for me, for I shall bring them good luck and guard them from evil for evermore." With that he disappeared forever, and his family were content for they believed the vision and knew him to be happy.

CURES AND CHARMS

ncient cures and charms were a gift, they were not
scientific, and many are still being performed today. They
relied largely on faith, be it in God, in the remedy itself,
or in the person administering it.

Cures were available for all sorts of ailments. They often
belonged to one particular person and would be passed on to a
chosen successor instructed to use them wisely.

It was believed that some people had natural healing powers,
for example, a seventh son or daughter, or best of all a seventh
son of a seventh son. Also a child born after its father had died
had the power to cure some illnesses.

A woman who married a man with the same surname, and to
whom she was otherwise not related, would have been thought to
have the cure for whooping cough. Recently someone in County
Tyrone, whose parents coincidentally had the same surname, told
me that when her mother first married, people would turn up at
the door seeking the cure and she had no idea what they were
talking about. When administered, the whopping cough cure must
have been rather a strange spectacle as it entailed the sick infant
being passed under a donkey's belly and over its back three times.

There were several different methods employed in curing mumps, a common childhood illness. These included the patient wearing the blinkers from a donkey and being led to a river where the water must be drunk direct, or across a south-flowing stream, or three times around a pig-sty. Another porcine cure for the illness involved the child having its head rubbed against the back of a pig while a phrase was called out in Irish "*muc, muc, seo dhuit do leici*" meaning "pig, pig, here are your mumps". The unfortunate pig would then catch the disease.

To cure childhood convulsions the clippings of the hair and nails of the infant were tied up in a linen cloth and placed under its cradle.

A treatment available for skin cancer was almost as dangerous as the disease itself. This relied on the use of a poultice, of which the main constituent was arsenic, being placed on the growth. The plaster caused agonising pain as it destroyed the tissue and many sufferers could not endure the pain or persist with the treatment. If the plaster was not removed then within two weeks it would fall off naturally taking a large part of the growth with it. Because of

the risks involved in using a proscribed poison, coupled with the advances in modern treatment for cancer, this practice has now completely died out.

On a lighter note, there were more cures for the common condition of warts than almost any other ailment. You could rub your hands in the forge water used by a blacksmith to cool his irons, or rub a freshly cut potato on the infected area and bury it in the garden; you could even rid yourself of warts by having someone "buy" them from you.

However, from personal experience my father still swears by this old charm for the cure of warts. About fifty years ago as a young boy in Armagh he was cured of twenty-eight warts on his hands using a charm involving a snail. He had to find a snail without looking for it and rub it over each wart three times. He then has to impale the snail on a thornbush, and when the snail fell off the warts would be gone. My father's warts had disappeared within a fortnight. Charm or coincidence?

A sty in the eye could be cured using the twig of a gooseberry bush with nine thorns. Each was in turn pointed to the sty and an Our Father, a Hail Mary and a Gloria said every time. The ritual was repeated daily for nine days to complete the cure. An altogether easier method simply required someone to say to the afflicted person "There is a sty in your eye" to which they would reply "You lie" and they would be cured.

Ringworm might be cured using the clay from where pallbearers walked or by a man or woman who never saw their father, blowing three times into the patient's mouth. In return he or she was required to be paid some small token or gift for the service.

In the past, as today, baldness in young men often caused much anxiety and any lengths would be gone to in an effort to rectify the condition. One of the old cures suggested the nightly use of an ointment made from the burned and ground embers of a sally tree mixed with hog's lard and turpentine. Even less savoury was a preparation to be rubbed on the scalp made from a jar of worms buried in a dung heap for a month. If the young man in question could not find romance I venture to suggest that his baldness may not have been the only reason! It is also safe to assume that neither of these treatments worked or else they would be widely available on pharmacy shelves today.

Freckles, another common source of discontent in appearance, were thought able to be removed, or at least faded, by regularly bathing the face in the blood of a bull or a hare. The more squeamish could use the distilled water of walnuts, and both remedies offered about the same effectiveness as the cure for baldness.

A sore throat could be cured by tying a stocking filled with hot potatoes around it, and an eel skin tied around a sprain would bring instant relief.

It was widely believed that the potent home-made poteen was a great cure-all, particularly for ague and rheumatism. It was said that if only the customs officers would leave these illicit stills alone "sure there wouldn't be a bit of sickness anywhere in Ireland".

One rather more distasteful remedy for toothache was to place a live frog in the mouth or chew on a frog's leg. Alternatively,

the two back legs of a frog would be soaked in water for two minutes, a spoon of pepper added, and the mixture boiled for ten minutes before being applied to the painful tooth.

A County Mayo cure for shingles involved the rubbing of a zinc-based ointment on the affected area of the patient accompanied by ten Hail Marys and ten Our Fathers. This was repeated for ten days at which time the painful blisters would have died away, but it would only work if the cure was performed by a man on a woman or vice versa.

The bleeding of wounds could reputedly be staunched using a cobweb or a tuft of fur from a hare, and a cut finger might be held in the smoke of a little sugar sprinkled on a lighted coal. A prayer often used for the healing of wounds went:

"The wound was red, the cut was deep, the flesh was sore:
But there'll be no more blood and no more pain,
Till the Virgin Mary bears a child again."

Often in the country there were only open fires available for heating and cooking and so burns were a common occurrence with many remedies on offer to heal them. Boiled sheep's suet and elder bark produced an ointment that could cure a burn without leaving a scar and the end of candles used at wakes were also said to be of great efficiency in curing burns.

In some areas it was thought that any man who ran his tongue over a lizard's back was given the power to cure a burn by in turn applying his tongue to the part affected. It was also believed in the West that if a person was licked by a species of lizard known as the "Mankeeper" they would never suffer from burns.

A simpler remedy was to blow upon the burn three times repeating the words:

> Two angels sat upon a stone,
> One was fire the other frost,
> Praise Father, Son and Holy Ghost.

To cure the common complaint of influenza some clay was scraped off the threshold, made into a paste and applied as a plaster to the chest. But to be effective, the clay had to be taken from the exact spot where a person first set foot on entering the house and spoke the salutation "God Bless All Here". It was held that those numerous blessings had given the clay a peculiar power to heal the chest and help the voice when it was affected. However, the holy power only worked on true believers for it was by God's faith they would be made whole.

For epilepsy, nine pieces of a dead man's skull, ground to a powder and mixed with a decoction of wall rue, was said to work wonders. A spoonful of this mixture was given to the patient every morning until the whole potion was swallowed. None of it was to be left or else the dead man would come back to look for the pieces of his skull, which would have undone any good effected by the charm.

Madness, in its milder forms, could be cured by giving the person three substances not procured by human means and not made by human hand. These were honey, milk and salt and they were given to the patient to be drunk from a sea-shell before sunrise.

The most gruesome remedy I uncovered was reserved for the treatment of varicose veins which would be cured if the affected area was rubbed with the hand of a recently hanged man.

Perhaps more of a black magic spell than a charm, this ritual claimed to give the user complete invisibility. You would take a raven's heart and split it open with a black-handled knife, making three cuts and placing a black bean in each. You then had to plant the heart and when the beans sprouted put one in your mouth and say: "By virtue of Satan's heart And by strength of my great Art I desire to be invisible." Invisibility would be guaranteed as long as the bean remained in your mouth.

Much as we might criticise the legal system from time to time, it certainly beats this old superstition for finding stolen goods. Two keys were placed on a sieve in the form of a cross, and two men held the sieve while a third made the sign of the cross on the forehead of the suspected party and called out their name loudly three times. If innocent, the keys remained stationary, but if guilty the keys revolved slowly around the sieve and there would be no doubt who the thief was. Naturally, the person found guilty had no right of appeal to the keys.

Given all this it probably seemed very wise to have a charm for safety available at every opportunity. Having plucked ten blades of yarrow, and cast the tenth away as tithe to the spirits, you would put the remaining nine in your stocking, under the right foot when going on a journey. Evil would have no power over you and you would arrive safely at your destination.

To make money without working you had to kill a black cock after nightfall and go to a fork in a road where a murderer was buried. Then you threw the dead bird over your left shoulder, in the name of the devil, while holding a coin in your hand. Ever after, no matter how much you spent, you would always find the same coin unspent in your pocket. It seems plausible to suggest that this may have died out for two reasons; the first being something of a scarcity of murderers buried at forks in the road, and secondly the diminishing value of coinage.